BEADED ANIMALS
in jewelry

LACIS publishes and distributes books specifically related to the textile arts, focusing on the subjects of lace and lace making, costume, embroidery, needlepoint and hand sewing.

Other LACIS books of interest:

For a complete list of LACIS titles please write to:

LACIS, 3136 Adeline Street, Berkeley, CA 94705, USA

BEADED ANIMALS
in jewelry

by

Letty Lammens & Els Scholte

LACIS
PUBLICATIONS
Berkeley, California 94703

*With thanks to all those who have assisted
in any way: W. Lammens, W. J. Scholte,
Kreat Automation and Kralerlei.*

Translated from the Dutch title
DIERENSIER GEREGEN KRALENSETS
Originally published by Cantecleer bv, de Bilt

© 1990 Uitgeverij Cantecleer bv de Bilt
© 1994 English text, Kangaroo Press

Photography: Studio Koppelman, Maarssen
Illustrations: Martin Paris
Design: Karel van Laar, de Bilt
English translation: Tina Llowarch

LACIS PUBLICATIONS
3163 Adeline Street
Berkeley, California 94706

ISBN-916896-61-7
This edition first published in 1994
Reprinted in 1995 and 1997

PUBLISHER'S NOTE:
Reflecting the international interest in beadwork, this publisher acknowledges the
British spelling of *jewellery* and *colour* which are used throughout the text rather than
the more accepted spelling of *jewelry* and *color* in the US.

Contents

1 *Animal pieces made with wooden beads*

Introduction

A number of specialised beading techniques, using metal beading wire, are required to make the different animals in this book. We recommend that you read and work through the sections on beading techniques before attempting the actual projects.

The animals in this book fall into three categories:
- *Endangered species:* penguin, elephant, several varieties of butterflies and of course the whale;
- *Domestic animals:* including a cat, dog and pig;
- *Frightening animals:* including a snake, bee, scorpion and spider.

We chose the spider as the linking thread throughout this book because we enjoyed making and wearing it.

The authors

2 *Materials and equipment*

Materials and equipment

- Small beads, 2 mm, in various colours
- Medium beads, 3 mm, in various colours
- Large beads, 5 mm, in various colours
- Bugle beads in various sizes and colours
- Thin metal, copper, silver and/or nylon-coated beading wire, 0.20 to 0.40 mm ('tigertail')
- Scissors with sharp points
- Flat-nosed ribbed pliers (the ribs are important for getting a firm grip on the beading wire)
- Round tube with a diameter of approx. 0.5 cm (3/8"), for example the end of a crochet hook, used to shape tubular beaded cords
- In some of the patterns you can use a variety of different sized beads, for example pearls 0.3 to 0.4 mm
- Brooch pins in various sizes
- Cord
- Eyepins and headpins
- Crochet cotton size 0.30
- Wooden beads
- Earring fittings or clips
- Metal wire (0.8 mm)
- Key rings, clasps, caps, decorative beads, perforated disc earrings, etc.

Guidelines

With the very thin metal wire used for this type of beading it is important to keep the wire taut, but not too tight. Try to avoid getting knots or loops in the wire, as too many knots and kinks can weaken it. If you do get a loop, gently uncoil the wire in the direction of the loop and smooth it over with your finger-nail.

All the patterns have been made using metal wire, as it gives the best results and makes it possible to position the animals to stand or sit or curl their tails, et cetera.

Spiders have been used as a symbol to indicate the degree of difficulty of each pattern. One spider indicates a simple pattern suitable for beginners, 2 spiders are a little more difficult, 3 spiders are for more advanced beaders.

The materials you will need are listed on page 9. Each pattern specifies only the size of the beads and the quantity necessary to make that particular design together with the length and thickness of the beading wire.

piece of beading wire is threaded with a row of beads, e.g. when making an ear (Fig. 3-1); 'double strand' means that two pieces of wire are threaded through a row of beads, e.g. when making a leg (Fig. 3-2).

The number of beads required for each pattern is specified, particularly useful when purchasing wooden beads or larger beads. As single beads are usually more expensive to purchase, it is more economical to buy the correct number. You don't have to stick to the sizes suggested, but remember that the larger the beads the larger the animal will be. In some cases you may find that the shape of the design is improved by using the back of a crochet hook to give the animal a more rounded finish.

1	

Single strand of wire

2	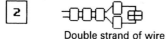

Double strand of wire

3 *Wiring symbols*

The finish of each article will generally depend on what the article is to be used for. Earrings will need hangers or clips, brooches will need a brooch pin or perforated disc brooch base.

The patterns will occasionally specify a single strand of wire or a double strand of wire. 'Single strand' means that one

Beading techniques

Setting-up

Thread 3 beads onto a piece of wire and push into the centre (see Fig. 4-1). Following Fig. 4-2 bend the wire back, bringing beads 2 and 3 under bead 1. In the next step (see Fig. 4-3) take wire b and push through beads 3 and 2. Wires a and b cross over in beads 2 and 3. Pull wires a and b gently but firmly. Continue working using wires a and b.

The number of beads to be used will always be indicated in each pattern—the 3 beads used here are only used as an example. Using this pattern, work can be started at the tail of the animal, as in the scorpion, the spider and the crab. It can also be used to start at the mouth of the animal, for example the pig, the elephant and the cat.

This way of setting up will be referred to where necessary in the various designs.

Flat beading technique

Flat beading is a relatively simple technique, quite often used for designs such as butterflies and for the tails of some designs.

We have created a simple design, the swordfish, to practise the flat beading technique.

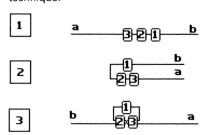

4 *Setting up*

Practice piece—the swordfish (page 12)
You will need
- 219 small beads, 2 mm (68 yellow, 151 orange)
- 1 medium bead, 3 mm (black)
- 1 m beading wire, 0.25 mm

Method (Fig. 6)
Start with setting up. Rows 2 and 3 are connected using the flat beading technique. Thread 1 bead to one of the wires of row 2. Bend the wire as shown in Fig. 5-1. The wire without the bead is taken through the bead in row 3 (Fig. 5-2). Both wires need to be pulled firmly but gently to enable row 3 to fit directly against row 2. This is the start of the swordfish (Fig. 6). Continue by making row 4, threading 2 beads onto the left wire. Bend this wire as shown in the pattern. The right wire— the wire without a bead—is taken through the beads of row 4. Repeat these rows following the pattern to row 12 inclusive. Remember to bead the eye in row 7.

The wire coming out of the left side of row 12 will form row 13. The wire coming out of the right side of row 12 will form the in-going wire of the first fin. After making the fin, and returning the wire around the last bead, the wire is taken through row 13.

The fin on the left side is made in a

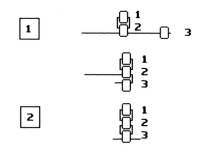

5 *Flat beading technique*

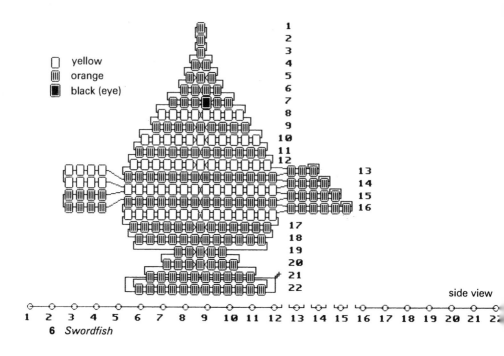

- ☐ yellow
- ▥ orange
- ■ black (eye)

1
2
3
4
5
6
7
8
9
10
11
12
13
14
15
16
17
18
19
20
21
22

side view

1 2 3 4 5 6 7 8 9 10 11 12 13 14 15 16 17 18 19 20 21 22

6 *Swordfish*

different way to the fin on the right side. The left wire coming out of row 13 forms the first fin on the left side. The wire coming out of the fin forms row 14. The right wire coming out of row 13 forms the in-going wire of the right fin. The wire coming from the fin is taken through row 14. Continue working, following the pattern to row 22, inclusive.

Finish the two wires as follows: take the left wire through row 21. The wires coming out of rows 21 and 22 are twisted together. See also the section on Finishing (page 16).

U-technique (Fig. 7)

This technique is used mainly for the so called 'double designs', for example the

scorpion on page 50, where the ribbed, slightly irregular effect is perfectly suited to the scorpion design. This technique is not as strong as the V-technique.

The beads in the upper layer lie directly above the beads in the lower layer. The flat beading technique gives a flat finish, but the U-technique adds an extra dimension by staggering the rows, making an upper and lower layer in the design. This is achieved by bending the wire so that each row is above or beneath the previous row, creating a U-effect. This can be seen in the side view, Fig. 7-1.

Patterns in U-technique

Each pattern in the U-technique shows the upper and lower layers separately. Both the upper and lower layers consist of a number of squares: the beads. Each bead's colour is indicated on the pattern by a special symbol. Double lines be-

12

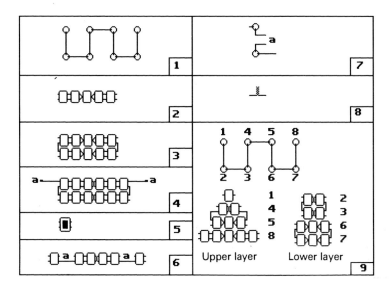

7 *U-technique*

tween the beads mean that the beads are connected to each other with two wires (see Fig. 7-2). The diagonal lines in the row indicate that the wires cross.

The connections between the rows need explaining. The example in Figure 7-9 is worked from the lower view; the upper view is done in the same manner. When the wire from one row is connected to the wire from another row, continue working this row on the lower layer. If the diagram shows a wire coming from a row that is not connected, that wire is worked into the upper layer of the following row (see Fig. 7-3). A diagram showing a wire that is slightly longer and ending in a black square means that before the wire is taken to the upper side it is used to make an ear or a leg. This will be indicated with a letter matching the ear or the leg (see Fig. 7-4).

The eyes are always pictured larger and are usually made with a medium bead. The same symbol is always used (see Fig. 7-5).

A space in the diagram, as if a row has been omitted, means that there is no row of beads—mostly this is done to make the article more flexible. A space in a row of beads, as if a bead is missing, means that an ear or a leg is to be made at that point as part of that row (see Fig. 7-6). A letter in the opening indicates the particular ear or leg.

The numbers at the side of the diagram indicate the order in which the rows are worked. The row numbers for the lower and upper views correspond to the side view (see Fig. 7-9).

Looking at the side of the work you will be able to see the wire in the work as it appears in the side view in Figure 7-9. The row numbers at the bottom of the side view correspond to the row numbers for the lower layer.

These instructions apply to the upper layer as well. The wires in the side view will occasionally have an opening (see Fig. 7-7); these are the wires that end in the lower and upper views of the diagram with a black square, the place to make an ear or leg. This also has a letter

13

indicating the ear or leg.
Figure 7-8 shows how to finish the wires, by twisting them together.

Practising the U-technique

This is used as an example only.
First set up rows 1 and 2, then start row 3 by threading onto the left wire. Bend the wire so that row 3 is next to row 2. Take the right wire through row 3 and pull gently but firmly. Thread all the beads for row 4 onto the left wire. Bend the wire so that row 4 is above row 3. Take the right wire through row 4 and pull the wire gently but firmly. Thread all the beads for row 5 on to the left wire. Bend the wire so that row 5 is next to row 4. Take the right wire through row 5 and pull gently but firmly. Repeat to row 8 inclusive, creating a side view as seen in Fig. 7-9.

V-technique (Fig. 8)

This technique is used mainly for the designs with a hollow centre, e.g. the pig, and gives a compact, tight finish. A design made using the V-technique is stronger than one made using the U-technique.
With the U-technique the rows of beads are worked on top of each other, while with the V-technique the upper and lower layers are worked diagonally. In effect each row is half a bead below the next (see Fig. 8-1).

Patterns in V-technique

Each pattern in the V-technique shows the upper and lower layers separately. Both the upper and lower layers consist of a number of squares: the beads. Each bead's colour is indicated on the patterns by a special symbol.
Double lines between the beads mean that the beads are connected with two wires (see Fig. 8-2).
The connections between the rows need explaining. This example is taken from the lower view; the upper view is worked in the same way. If the wire coming from the row is drawn as not connecting, then that wire goes to the upper side in the next row (see Fig. 8-3). If the wire is

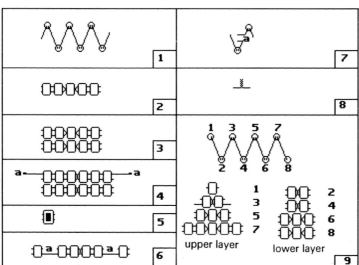

upper layer   lower layer

longer and ends in a black square, this means that before the wire goes to the upper side it is used to make an ear or a leg, et cetera. There will always be a letter to indicate the pictured ear or leg (see Fig. 8-4). The eyes are always shown large and a medium size bead is usually used. The same symbol is always used (see Fig. 8-5).

A space in the drawing, as if a row has been skipped, means that there is no row of beads at that point; this is done to give flexibility to the article. A space in a row of beads, as if a bead is missing, indicates that at that point an ear or leg must be made as part of that row (see Fig. 8-6). A letter in the opening indicates the particular ear or leg.

The numbers at the side of the pattern indicate the order in which the rows are to be beaded. The row numbers in the lower and upper view correspond to the numbers in the side view.

Looking at the side of the work the wire can be seen going in the direction indicated on the diagram. The row numbers at the bottom of the side view correspond to the row numbers for the lower layer.

These instructions also apply to the upper layer. The wires in the side view will occasionally have an opening (see Fig. 8-7); these are the wires from the lower or upper views of the pattern that end in a black square: the place where an ear or a leg is to be made. This also has a letter indicating the ear or leg. Figure 8-8 shows that the wires are finished by twisting them together.

Practising the V-technique

This is used as an example only.
First set up rows 1 and 2, and start row 3 by threading onto the left wire. The wire is bent so that row 3 is diagonally above row 2. Take the right wire through row 3 and pull gently but firmly. Thread all the beads for row 4 onto the left wire. Bend the wire so that row 4 is diagonally under

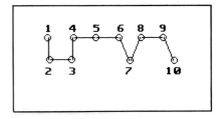

8a *Combined techniques*

row 3. Take the right wire through row 4 and pull gently but firmly. Thread all the beads for row 5 on to the left wire. Bend the wire so that row 5 is diagonally above row 4. Take the right wire through row 5 and pull gently but firmly. Repeat to row 8 inclusive, which creates the side view as seen in Fig. 8-9.

Combined techniques

These three techniques can be used together, as in the example of a side view given in Fig. 8a. Here, in rows 1 to 4 inclusive the U-technique is used, in rows 4 to 6 inclusive the flat technique, in rows 6 to 8 inclusive the V-technique, rows 8 and 9 the flat technique, while rows 9 and 10 return to the V-technique.

Using beading wire

For each basic pattern only the length of wire needed is specified. The thickness of the wire is a matter of personal choice, although we have found a wire of 0.25 mm thickness suitable for most projects. When using larger beads, however, it is advisable to use a thicker wire. For example, the dachshund on page 34 uses 0.5 mm beads and a thicker wire (0.30 mm) was found to be more effective.

The choice between the different wires is a personal preference. Four types of wire can be used: copper, brass, plastic-coated metal wire (tigertail) and silver wire, the last being more easily broken than the other three. The choice of wire will depend on the design to be made and the available colour combinations.

Broken wires

If the wire has been pulled too hard, or has kinked or twisted, or has had to be unpicked, it can occasionally break. Our advice, if the design is not too far advanced, is to start again with a new wire. If, however, the wire breaks when the design is almost completed, all is not lost. Take a new piece of wire and attach it to the broken end. Twist the two pieces together as you would for finishing the wire and push the twisted end into the work. Continue working with the new wire. This wire will not be quite as strong as the original wire, however, so keep this in mind when the wire needs to be pulled tight.

Finishing (Fig. 9)

When a design has been completed two pieces of wire remain. Cut them approximately 2 cm (3/4") from the last bead and using the flat-nosed pliers twist them securely together. Cut the twist approximately 0.5 cm (3/8") from the work and bend back. This is shown in Fig. 9-1. In some designs it is not possible to finish the wires this way. The alternative is to take one wire and pull it through the previous row, so that both ends are together on one side of the work. Cut the wires approximately 2 cm (3/4") from the last bead and with the flat-nosed pliers twist them together (see Fig. 9-2). Both methods of finishing the wire are used in this book.

9 *Finishing*

Endangered animals

Crocodile (page 31)

You will need
• 244 small beads, 2 mm (95 light green, 120 dark green, 29 brown)
• 2 medium beads, 3 mm (dark brown)
• 1 m beading wire

Method (Fig. 10)
The crocodile is one of the most often made of the beaded animals. This pattern has a slight variation on the usual crocodile; the mouth is made in an open position.
Start by making the mouth using row 1 (upper) and the flat beading method to row 7 inclusive. The lower part of the mouth will be made at a later stage and individually fastened. Do not forget to bead both eyes in row 5.
Starting at row 8 use the U-technique which will bring row 8 under row 7, row 9 next to row 8 and row 10 above row 9, et cetera. Continue with this technique to row 41 inclusive. In the connection

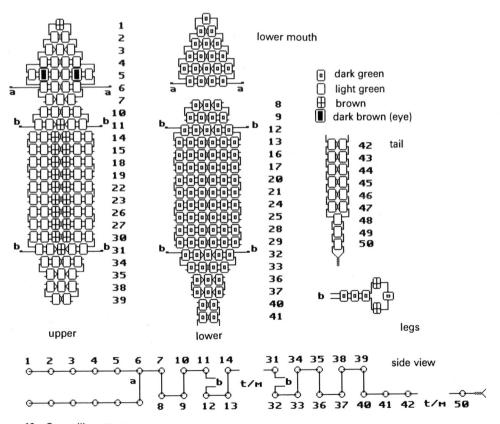

10 *Crocodile pattern*

between row 11 (upper) and row 12 (lower) make both front legs. Wire b from row 11 (upper) will form the leg. To make the leg thread 3 dark green, 1 brown, 1 dark green and 1 brown bead. Take the wire back through the 3 dark green beads. Do the same on the other side and complete row 12 (lower). The back legs are made between the connection of row 31 (upper) and row 32 (lower). They are made the same as the front legs. From row 41 (lower) to row 50 inclusive work in the flat technique; this makes the tail.

The lower part of the mouth is made next: a piece of six rows, starting at row 1 using the flat technique. The ends of the wire that remain when row 6 is finished are used to attach the lower part of the mouth to the upper part. In the pattern this is indicated by the letter a.

Finishing
Finish all loose wires. Bend the legs into shape. Curl the tail around and open the mouth.

Blue crocodile set (page 19)
You will need
- Medium beads, 3 mm (black, light blue and cobalt blue)
- Beads, 5 mm, for eyes (black)
- Beading wire 0.3 and 0.8 mm
- Nylon thread 0.25 mm
- Crimps and calottes
- Clasp
- 2 earhangers
- 60 pearls, 4 mm, for earrings (light blue)
- 16 strass beads no. 5
- 4 strass beads no. 8
- 32 pearls, 8 mm, for necklace (blue)
- 13 blue beads

Method
Using the 3 mm and 5 mm beads make four crocodiles, two for the necklace and two for the earrings.

Necklace
Attach a calotte and a crimp to the nylon thread. Bead 1 blue bead, 5 blue pearls, 1 bead, 4 pearls, 1 bead, 3 pearls, 1 bead, 1 pearl, 1 strass no. 8, 1 pearl, 1 bead, 1 crocodile (from tail to mouth), 1 bead, 1 pearl, 1 strass no 8, 1 pearl and 1 bead. This last blue bead is the centre. Continue, threading everything in reverse order (except for the blue centre bead). Attach the clasp to the calottes.

Earrings
Take a piece of wire (0.8 mm) approximately 20 cm (8") long. Form this into a circle by bending around an empty container. Make a ring on one end and thread 4 times: 3 pearls, 1 strass bead no. 5, ending with 3 pearls. Thread through the crocodile and reverse the beading. Make a ring at the other end and fasten the eyes together to the earhanger.

Red crocodile set (back cover)
You will need
- Bugle beads, 2 mm, for the necklace (red and black)
- Beads, 2 mm, for the crocodiles (red and black)
- Beads, 3 mm, for the eyes (black)
- 4 caps (gold)
- Clasp
- 10 strass beads (black)
- 16 pearls, 8 mm (red)
- 3 beads (black)
- Beading wire 0.25, 0.30 and 0.80 mm
- Crochet cotton no. 30 (black)
- Headpins
- Two pieces of chain (3 and 5 cm)
- Brooch pin with 3 holes
- 2 earhangers

Method
Using the red and black beads (2 mm and 3 mm) make five crocodiles—two for the necklace, two for the earrings and one for the brooch.

> **Plate 1** *Blue crocodile set*

11 *Elephant earring*

Necklace

To make the beaded cord necklace
thread * 4 black and 2 red bugle beads in
the first ring and repeat from *. Make
two pieces of cord each 20 cm (8") long.
In the necklace pictured one piece of the
cord was beaded by a left-handed person and the other by a right-handed
person, causing the red twist to appear
to run in opposite directions. Finish both
pieces at the top with 1 cap, 1 strass
bead and 1 red pearl. Twist the end into a
ring and attach the clasp. Finish both
pieces at the bottom with 1 cap, 1 strass
bead and 1 red pearl. Before closing the
ring attach the crocodile between rows
34 and 35 to the ring. Between the
crocodiles make a decorative piece from
1 red pearl, 1 strass bead, 1 black bead,
1 strass bead and one red pearl. Attach
this piece between row 34 and 35 of the
crocodiles. Close the rings.

Earrings

Thread on to eyepin 1 red pearl, 1 crocodile (from mouth to tail) and 1 red pearl.
Twist the end into a ring and attach the
earhanger. Make second earring in the
same manner.

Brooch

Thread on to headpin 1 red pearl, 1
crocodile (from mouth to tail) and 1 red
pearl. Twist end into a ring and attach to
the middle hole of the brooch pin.
Thread on to 2 headpins 1 red pearl, 1
strass bead, 1 black bead, 1 strass bead
and 1 red pearl. Twist into ring. Attach
one ring to a piece of chain 5 cm (2")
long and one ring to a piece of chain 3
cm (1¼") long. Attach one chain by
opening a link to the left hole in the
brooch pin and one chain to the right
hole in the brooch pin.

Elephant (page 31)

You will need
- 304 small beads, 2 mm (286 grey, 18 beige)
- 2 medium beads, 3 mm (black)
- 1.5 m beading wire

Method (Fig. 12)
The elephant is quite simple to make. Following the pattern, use the setting-up technique for rows 1 and 2. Continue working in the V-technique to row 24 inclusive. In the connection between rows 24 and 25 the elephant's tusks are made (from base to tip). The tusk is made of 9 beads; make a loop with the wire around the 9th bead and take it back through the beads to the body. Repeat this to make the second tusk.

Rows 26 and 27 are made in the V-technique. Rows 27 and 28 (upper) are connected using the flat technique. These two rows give the head its rounded shape. The eyes are beaded in row 30. Continue using the V-technique to row 37 inclusive. The ears are beaded between rows 37 and 38. When row 37 is finished, thread 29 beads on to both sides of the wire then make row 38. Twist the ears several times.

Row 38 (upper) and row 39 (upper) are connected using the flat technique; row 40 (lower) using the V-technique. The two wires can now be twisted together and pushed into the head, or pulled through the holes in the brooch pin if you are making the brooch.

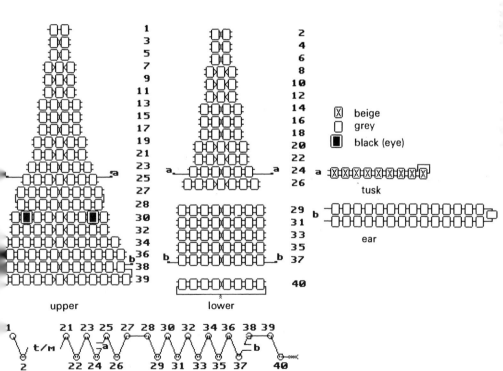

12 *Elephant pattern*

Finishing
Finish all loose wires. Bend the ears, the trunk and the tusks into shape.

Elephant set (front cover)
You will need
- Pearls, 3 mm (grey and pink)
- Beads for eyes (black)
- 6 caps (anthracite)
- Clasp
- Beading wire, 0.30 and 0.80 mm
- Three-stranded cord (pink)
- Thin cord (grey with silver)
- 4 pearls, 8 mm (pink)
- 2 pearls, 12 mm (anthracite)
- 4 strass beads, 6 mm
- 2 large perforated disc earring clips, 3 cm
- Nylon thread 0.25 mm
- Crochet cotton no. 30
- 4 small pieces of wire for fastening

Method
Using the 3 mm pearls make five pink elephants with grey tusks. Leave the loose wires unfinished. Three of the elephants will be used for the necklace and two for the earrings.

Necklace
To make the beaded cord necklace thread: * 4 anthracite pearls and 1 pink pearl in the first ring, and repeat from *. Bead two pieces of necklace each approximately 20 cm (8") long. Finish these with a cap and attach the clasp at the top.
The centre part of the necklace consists of two decorative beaded sections and the centrepiece with three elephants. For the decorative beaded sections thread on to wire: 1 pink pearl 8 mm, 1 strass bead, 1 grey pearl 12 mm, 1 strass bead and 1 pink pearl 8 mm. Twist wire into a ring at both ends and attach to beaded necklace. To make the centrepiece take a piece of pink cord approximately 40 cm (16") long and wind the grey cord around it. Tie three evenly spaced knots in the

cord. Finish the cord ends with the caps and fasten it to the beaded sections. The three elephants are attached to the three knots in the cord with the wires previously left unfinished. Finish the wires by very carefully working them into the knots.

Earrings
For each earring you will need pink cord approximately 12 cm (5") long with grey cord the same length wound around it. Make a knot in the centre of the cord and attach the elephant to the knot with the unfinished wires. Attach this to the earring base.

Peacock butterfly (page 31)

You will need
- Small beads, 2 mm (39 brown, 36 black, 204 orange, 84 grey, 16 blue, 24 yellow, 34 white)
- Beading wire, 25 cm (10") to make the body
- 4 pieces beading wire, approx. 60 cm (24") for the wings

Method (Fig. 13)
The butterflies in this book are all made using the flat technique, making them very suitable for children to make.
The butterfly is made up of several separate parts joined together.
Start by making the lower part of the body. The body consists of 12 rows. The two wires coming out of row 12 will form the antennae. Thread 1 bead on to the right wire and fasten it approximately 1.5 cm (5/8") above row 12. Do the same with the left wire. Finish all loose wires. The upper and lower wings are made following the pattern. The patterns on the right of the diagram describe the order of beading and are twisted a quarter turn. The patterns on the left depict the wings as they are to be attached.

> **Plate 2** *Animals and insects made with wooden beads*

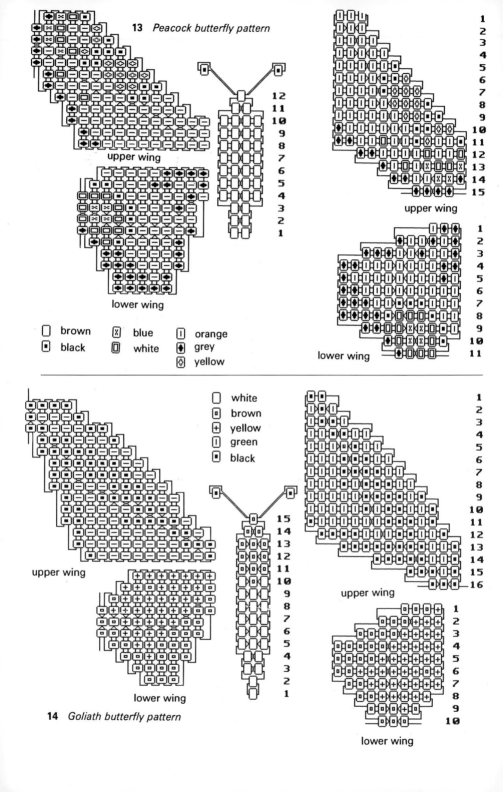

13 *Peacock butterfly pattern*

upper wing

lower wing

1 2 3 4 5 6 7 8 9 10 11 12

☐ brown   ☒ blue   ◫ orange
▣ black   ▯ white   ◉ grey
             ⊗ yellow

upper wing

lower wing

1 2 3 4 5 6 7 8 9 10 11 12 13 14 15

1 2 3 4 5 6 7 8 9 10 11

☐ white
▣ brown
⊞ yellow
▯ green
▣ black

upper wing

lower wing

14 *Goliath butterfly pattern*

upper wing

lower wing

15 14 13 12 11 10 9 8 7 6 5 4 3 2 1

1 2 3 4 5 6 7 8 9 10 11 12 13 14 15 16

1 2 3 4 5 6 7 8 9 10

Row 1 of each wing is attached to to the body with a separate piece of beading wire. Use a small piece of beading wire to connect the two parts of each wing.

Page 31 shows several other butterflies. With the exception of the Goliath butterfly (described below) all the butterflies are made using this pattern and varying the colours.

Goliath butterfly (page 31)

You will need
- 428 small beads, 2 mm (79 brown, 128 black, 78 yellow, 120 green, 23 white)

Method (Fig. 14)
This butterfly is made using the directions for the peacock butterfly. The wings and body, however, use different colour combinations and a different number of rows, as shown in the pattern opposite.

Whale (page 31)

You will need
- 308 small beads, 2 mm (231 grey, 77 pearl white)
- 2 medium beads, 3 mm (black)
- 1.25 m (1¼ yd) and 2 x 30 cm (12") beading wire

Method (Fig. 16)
The whale is made up of several parts:

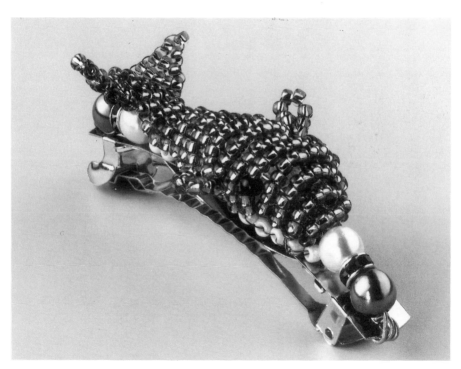

15 *Whale hair clip*

the body, the lower part of the jaw and the two uplifted tail flukes.

Start by making the two side pieces of the tail. Made separately, each consists of 5 rows using the flat beading technique; they are joined to the 'tail' of the body.

The first tail fluke is worked on the 1.25 m (1¼ yd) length of beading wire (for the entire whale) and is worked from the centre, using the pattern for the flat technique (page 11). For the second fluke use a 30 cm (12") piece of wire and work in a similar way as for the first. The first fluke is used on the left side and the second on the right side.

Using wire a of the left fluke and wire b of the right fluke, bead the first five rows following the flat technique. The pattern shows a space between the flukes and row 1; actually the flukes need to be pulled close against row 1, fitting snugly against the body.

Wire b will now be at the left side of the work and wire a at the right side of row 5. The long wire c which comes out of the left fluke is used to bead row 6. Wire b coming from row 5 is taken through bead x of the left fluke, and finished off in row 6 (see P and Q in diagram). The long wire coming from the right side of row 5 is taken through bead x of the right fluke—attaching it to the body at the same time—and taken through row 6. The short wire d coming from the right fluke is finished off in row 6. From the side view it looks as though the flukes are not attached to the whale but this gives a wrong impression. The diagram shows the five rows of each fluke and shows the connection between rows 5 and 6 via bead x of the back fluke.

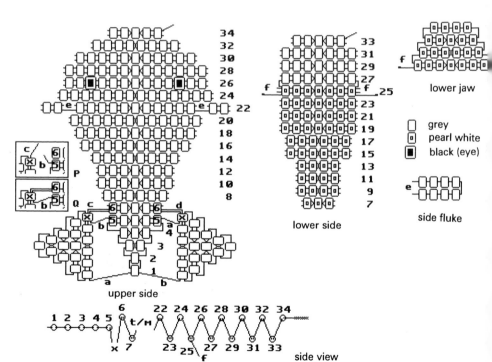

16   *Whale pattern*

> **Plate 3** *Blue whale set*

Continue working using the V-technique up to and including row 22. In row 22 the two flukes are made after the first two beads (on both sides), by making two loops of eight beads each. Take the wire back through the rest of the row and through the two beads under the flukes. Twist the flukes around twice. The rows at the top of the whale have a lot more beads, giving a nice rounded shape to the head of the whale.

Continue using the V-technique up to and including row 34 (the eyes are beaded in row 26). From row 27 change to the grey beads for the lower part. Take one wire back through the last row of the lower side. The two wires are then finished together. The last part to be made is the lower side of the jaw. Using the other 30 cm (12") piece of wire, bead 4 rows using the flat technique, starting at the lower side. The wires coming out of the lower jaw are used to attach the jaw to the underneath of the whale in row 25.

Finishing
Finish off all loose wires. Bend the tail and side fins into shape.

Blue whale set (page 27)
You will need
- Small beads, 2 mm, for the small whale (turquoise and pearl white)
- 2 medium beads, 3 mm, for the eyes (black)
- Medium beads, 3 mm (turquoise and pearl white)
- Large beads, 4 mm for the eyes (black)
- Beading wire 0.25, 0.30 and 0.80 mm
- 2 white caps and 2 silver caps
- 4 decorative caps
- 8 white strass beads no. 5
- 10 decorative pearls
- Pair of earring hangers
- Eyepins
- Clasp
- Crochet cotton no. 30 (white)

- 2 pearls no. 4 (white)

Method
Following the pattern make four whales using 3 mm beads in turquoise and pearl white. The eyes are made using 4 mm beads in black. Two of these whales are for the earrings. Also make a small whale using 2 mm beads in the same colours as the large whales, using 0.25 mm wire.

Necklace
Make two pieces of beaded cord each about 15 cm (6") long, using six beads in each circle. Bead as pattern: * 2 turquoise, 2 pearl white, 1 turquoise, 1 pearl white, repeat from *. Finish each piece with caps, decorative pearls and a clasp on one side. Attach a ring to each side of the two large whales and the small whale and string a decorative piece consisting of pearls and strass beads between each whale.

Earrings
Push an eyepin through the whale from bottom to top. Close the eye around the last row of beads. At the top of the eyepin thread 2 decorative pearls and a strass bead, loop the end of the eyepin into a ring and attach the earring hangers.

Grey whale set (Fig. 17)
You will need
- Medium beads, 3 mm (pearl white and grey)
- Large beads, 4 mm, for the eyes (black)
- Beading wire, 0.30 and 0.80 mm
- Gold-coloured clasp
- 4 crimps and calottes (gold coloured)
- 2 small decorative caps
- 2 large decorative caps
- Hairclip
- 1 pearl, 14 mm (grey)
- 2 pearls, 12 mm (white)
- 8 strass beads (black)
- 34 pearls, 8 mm (grey)

17 *Grey whale set*

- 34 pearls, 8 mm (grey)
- 32 pearls, 8 mm (white)
- Nylon beading thread no. 25

Method
Using the medium and large beads make three whales, two for the necklace and one for the hairclip.

Hairclip
For the hairclip cut a piece of 0.80 mm beading wire approximately 20 cm (8") long. Attach the wire to one side of the hairclip. Thread on: 1 grey pearl, 1 strass bead, 1 white pearl, 1 whale, 1 white pearl, 1 strass bead and 1 grey pearl. Fasten wire to the other side of the clip.

Necklace
Make two pieces of necklace, using 1 grey and 1 white pearl alternately. Finish both ends with a crimp and a calotte. Fasten the clasp to the top. The rest of the necklace is made up of three pieces,

each on a separate piece of beading wire (0.80 mm). The rings are joined together. Two pieces made from: 1 grey pearl, 1 strass bead, 1 white pearl, 1 whale, 1 white pearl, 1 strass bead and 1 grey pearl. The middle piece is made from: 1 white pearl 12 mm, 1 decorative cap, 1 strass bead, 1 decorative cap, 1 grey pearl 14 mm, 1 decorative cap, 1 strass bead, 1 decorative cap and 1 white pearl 12 mm.

Penguin (page 31)

You will need
- 334 small beads, 2 mm (149 black, 4 yellow, 76 anthracite, 105 white)
- 2 medium beads, 3 mm (white)
- 1.5 m beading wire

Method (Fig. 19)
The penguin is started at the beak (rows

18 *Penguin pin*
19 *Penguin pattern*

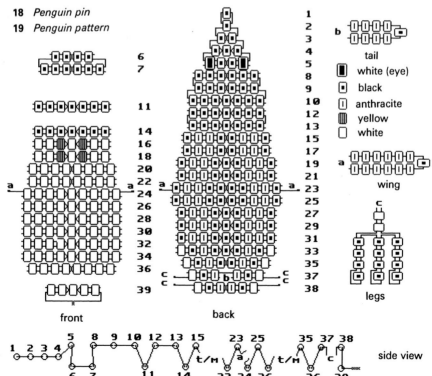

tail

■	white (eye)
•	black
□	anthracite
Ⅲ	yellow
☐	white

wing

legs

front

back

side view

> **Plate 4** *Beaded animals and insects*

1 to 5 inclusive) using the flat technique. The eyes are added in row 5 using the medium beads. Row 6 is made following the U-technique and is made under row 5. Rows 7 and 8 are also made using the U-technique. Row 9 is made following the flat technique, giving some flexibility to the neck. The connection between rows 10 and 11 and the connection between rows 11 and 12 are made using the V-technique. Between rows 12 and 13 a flat connection is made. Rows 13 to 23 inclusive are worked in the V-technique. The two wires coming out of row 23 are used to form the wings (see pattern) and after the wings are finished they are used together to form row 24 at the front. In row 24 the wires are pulled gently to even the work, the wings are twisted a full turn to loosen them from the body a little, then the wires of row 24 are pulled firm.

From row 24 continue working in the V-technique up to row 37 inclusive. The tail is made in the middle of row 37, starting from the b in the pattern. Thread the first three beads of row 37, nine beads for the tail and the last three beads onto the left wire. Take the right wire through the beads of row 37, but not through the beads of the tail. The two wires coming out of row 37 will form the legs (see pattern). After the legs are made the wires will form row 38 at the back. Row 38 is pulled gently, the legs are twisted a full turn to loosen them from the body a little, then the wires of row 38 are pulled firm to even the work. The two wires coming out of row 38 together form row 39 at the front.

Finishing
Finish all loose wires. Spread the toes forward on each leg. Adjust the wings and bend forward. Bend the head slightly forward.

Penguin pin (Fig. 18)
You will need
- Medium beads, 3 mm (cobalt blue, lilac, oil blue)
- 2 m (2½ yds) beading wire 0.30 mm
- Gold-coloured metal chain—2 pieces 4 cm (1½ ") long, one piece 2 cm (¾") long and one piece 3 cm (1¼") long
- 2 rings
- 2 bells (gold)
- Star (gold)
- Brooch pin with 3 holes

Method
Make a penguin using the 3 mm beads and attach it with a ring to a 4 cm (1½") chain. Attach the chain to the middle hole of the brooch pin. Attach the bells to the other 4 cm (1½") chain and the 3 cm (1¼") chain, then fasten these two pieces of chain to one ring and the ring to the left hole of the brooch pin. Attach the star to the 2 cm (¾") chain and the ring to the right hole of the brooch pin.

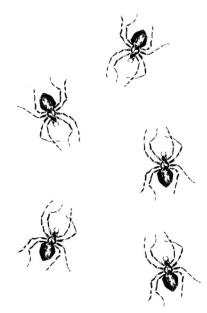

> **Plate 5** *Dachshund set*

Domestic animals

Dachshund (page 31)

You will need
- 279 small beads, 2 mm (274 brown, 5 black)
- 2 medium beads, 3 mm (black)
- 1.5 m (1½ yds) beading wire

Method (Fig. 20)
Start at the nose (rows 1 and 2) following the setting-up technique. Continue, using the V-technique to row 12 inclusive. In row 9 the eyes are beaded with the medium beads. The two wires coming out of row 12 form the ears (see pattern). When the ears have been made the two wires together form row 13 on the upper side. Row 13 is pulled gently, the ear is twisted a full turn to loosen it from the body, then row 13 is pulled firmly to even the work. The two wires coming out of row 13 go to the lower side and together form row 14. Repeat this up to and including row 16 (row 16 is on the lower side).

The connection between rows 16 and 17 is made in the flat technique. This creates the flexibility to move the head to different positions. The two wires coming out of row 17 are taken to the upper side and together form row 18. Continue working further in the V-technique to row 20 inclusive (upper).

Row 21 contains both front legs. With the right wire thread the first bead of row

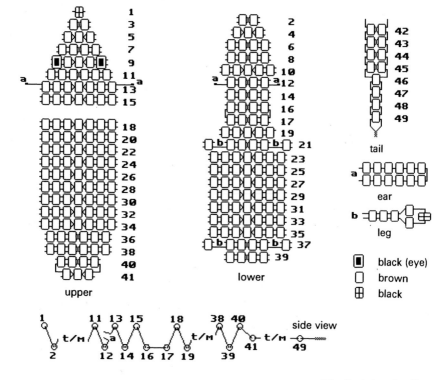

upper

lower

tail

ear

leg

■ black (eye)
☐ brown
⊞ black

side view

21. Make the leg following the pattern. With the left wire thread one bead and make the leg following the pattern. Thread the rest of the beads onto the left wire. Take the right wire through the beads on the left wire. The right wire also goes through the first bead of the left wire (the bead for the leg). Take the left wire through the first bead of the right wire (the bead for the leg). Continue working in the V-technique to row 36 inclusive (upper). Row 37 is made the same as row 21, to make both back legs. Continue working in V-technique to row 41 inclusive. The tail is made up to row 49 inclusive using the flat technique.

Finishing
Finish all loose wires. Make sure the legs are straight. Curl the tail. Push the ears into shape and bend the head up a little.

Dachshund set (page 33)
You will need
- Medium beads, 3 mm (black and bronze)
- Large beads, 4 mm, for the eyes (black)
- 61 pearls, 8 mm (salmon)
- Hairclip
- Beading wire 0.30 and 0.80 mm
- 14 strass beads no. 6 (brown)
- Clasp
- 2 crimps and calottes
- Nylon thread no. 25

Method
Using the medium and large beads make three dachshunds, two for the necklace, one for the hairclip.

Hairclip
Take a piece of beading wire (0.80 mm) approximately 20 cm (8") long. Attach one end to the hairclip. Thread 1 pearl, 1 dachshund, 1 pearl, 1 strass bead, 1 pearl. Fasten wire to the other end of the hairclip.

Necklace
Thread a crimp and a calotte onto beading wire then continue: 3 pearls, 1 strass bead, * 5 pearls, 1 strass bead, repeat from * twice, 5 pearls, 1 dachshund, 3 pearls, 1 strass bead, 2 pearls, 1 strass bead, 1 pearl, 1 strass bead, 1 pearl, 1 strass bead, 2 pearls, 1 strass bead, 3 pearls, 1 dachshund, * 5 pearls, 1 strass bead, repeat from * 3 times and finish with 3 pearls. Finish off.

Mouse

You will need
- 232 small beads, 2 mm (black)
- 2 medium beads, 3 mm (brown)
- 1 m (1 yd) beading wire

Method (Fig. 22)
The mouse is started at the nose, using the setting up technique for rows 1 and 2. Row 3 is made above row 2 using the V-technique. Row 4 is connected in the V-technique, but in this row do not tighten the wire, making a loop on either side instead (see Fig. 21-1). These loops are twisted several times (see Fig. 21-2) to make the whiskers. In the next two connections up to row 6 inclusive two more sets of whiskers are made. The rest of the mouse is made in the V-technique. In row 7 (upper) the eyes are beaded. Continue working to row 10 (lower) inclusive.
In row 11 (upper) make the ears, threading 6 beads on the left wire and 8 beads on the right wire. Take the left wire

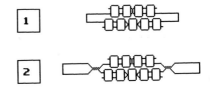

21 *Pattern for the mouse's whiskers*

Plate 7 *Mouse set*

<   **Plate 6**   *Green snake set*

through the last two beads of the right wire, skip the next 5 beads (these will form the ear) and through the first bead of the right wire. Lightly pull the wires. Take the right wire through the first bead of the left wire. Again, lightly pull the wires. Form the ears and tighten wires firmly.

Continue working in the V-technique to row 30 inclusive. Rows 31 to 44 inclusive form the tail (flat technique). Finish off.

Finishing
Finish all loose wires. Cut the loops for the whiskers, bend into shape and curl the tail.

Mouse set (page 37)
You will need
- Bugle beads, 2 mm, for the necklace (purple)
- Small beads, 2 mm, for the mice (lilac)
- 7 small beads, 2 mm, for the nose (pink)
- Medium beads, 3 mm, for the eyes (black)

- Beading wire 0.25, 0.30 and 0.80 mm
- Hairclip
- Pair of earring hangers
- Eyepins
- Brooch pin
- Crochet cotton no. 30 (purple)
- Clasp
- 4 caps (anthracite)
- 4 decorative caps
- 16 pearls, 4 mm (purple)
- 6 pearls, 8 mm (purple)
- 9 strass beads no. 4 (silver)
- 2 strass beads no. 6 (silver)
- Strass ball
- Lapel pin

Method
Following the pattern make seven mice, using the small and medium beads. Make the four mice for the necklace and earrings without whiskers to prevent skin irritation.

Necklace
Using the bugle beads make two beaded cords each 20 cm (8") long, 8 beads in

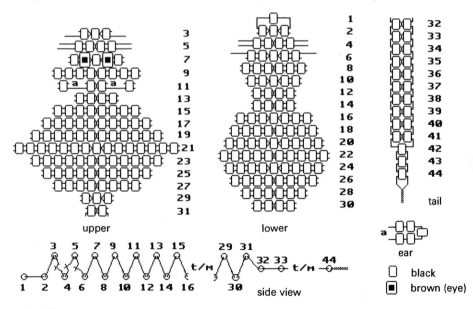

upper   lower

side view

ear

☐ black
■ brown (eye)

22 *Mouse pattern*

each row. To the top attach caps and decorative caps and a clasp. At the bottom fasten caps and decorative caps, 1 strass bead no. 4 and 1 pearl 4 mm. Join with two mice without whiskers and a middle section, which is made from 1 pearl 4 mm, 1 strass bead no. 4, 1 pearl 8 mm, 1 strass ball, 1 pearl 8 mm, 1 strass bead no. 4 and 1 pearl 4 mm.

Earrings
Take two mice without whiskers and fasten to headpins. Add decorative caps, strass beads and pearls similar to the necklace. Twist a ring into the end of the headpin and attach an earhanger.

Lapel pin
Take one mouse (with whiskers) and fasten to the lapel pin, adding decorative caps, strass beads and pearls similar to the necklace. Close with a cap.

Brooch
Take one mouse (with whiskers) and fasten to the brooch pin with 0.25 mm beading wire.

Hairclip
Take two mice (with whiskers). Attach beading wire to one end of the hairclip. Fasten mice and decorative caps, pearls and a strass bead to the beading wire. Attach other end of beading wire to clip.

Hedgehog (page 31)

You will need
- 106 small beads, 2 mm (94 dark brown, 12 black)
- 41 medium beads, 3 mm (38 dark brown, 3 black)
- 118 bugle beads (dark brown)
- 2 m (2 yds) beading wire

Method (Fig. 23)
Start making the hedgehog at the snout. Rows 1 to 13 inclusive are connected using the V-technique. Bead the eyes in row 9. The ears are made in row 13. Thread 1 bead onto the left wire (1st bead of row 13), then 5 beads for the ear and 7 beads for the rest of row 13. Onto

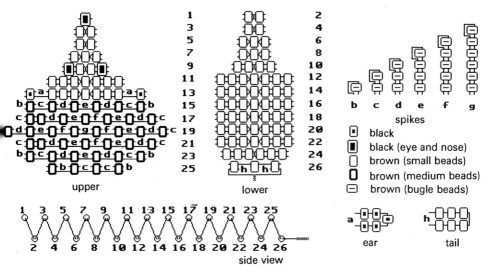

23 Hedgehog pattern

the right wire thread 1 bead (last bead of row 13), 5 beads for the ear. Take the wire through the 7 beads of the left wire, skip across the ear and take wire through the bead in front of the ear (the first bead of row 13). Take the left wire through the last bead of row 13. Pull the wires in row 13 and the ears will straighten up.

Rows 14 to 25 inclusive are made using the V-technique. In rows 15, 17, 19, 21, 23 and 25 (upper) the spikes are beaded. In these rows each bead is threaded through four times, therefore a medium sized bead is used (see pattern). Row 15 is made in the same way as row 14. On the right wire coming out of row 15 the first spike b is beaded (1 bugle bead); make a loop around this and take the wire back through the first bead of row 15. Between the first and second bead of row 15 make spike c (2 bugle beads); make a loop around the top bugle bead and take the wire through the second bead of row 15. Follow with spikes d, e, d and c, up to and including the sixth bead of row 15. Thread onto left wire 1 bugle bead, spike b, and take the wire through all six beads of row 15. In row 17 there is no spike between the first and second beads of the left side. Follow

24 *Pig hairclip*

pattern carefully for correct order of spikes, finishing spikes on row 25 (upper).

The tail is beaded in row 26 (lower). Make row 26 with the left wire, take the right wire through the last bead of the left wire, thread the 6 beads of the tail onto the right wire and take the wire through the first bead on the left wire.

Finishing
Finish all loose wires. Bend the snout slightly upward and push the ears into shape

Pig (page 31)

You will need
- 302 small beads, 2 mm (294 pink, 8 black)
- 1.5 m (1½ yd) beading wire

Method (Figs 25 and 26)
The pig is begun at the nose. Thread onto wire 1 pink, 1 black, 1 pink and 1 black bead following Fig. 26-1. Take the left wire through the right side of the second black bead (4) creating a circle (see Fig. 26-2). Twist the work a quarter twist to the left. The black bead with both wires coming out of it is now on the left (see Fig. 26-3). Take the top wire R and work through the other black bead (2, see Fig. 26-4). The two black beads, 2 and 4, form row 1. The star (*) in row 1 in the pattern is a reminder that although 2 beads are illustrated, 4 beads are actually used. Thread 3 pink beads onto the wire for row 2 (lower), and continue working in the V-technique to row 11 inclusive. The eyes are beaded in row 9. The connection between rows 11 and 12 is made using the flat technique. This enables the head to be more flexible. Bead row 12. The two wires coming out of row 12 are used to make the ears. Following Fig. 26-5, thread 13 beads onto

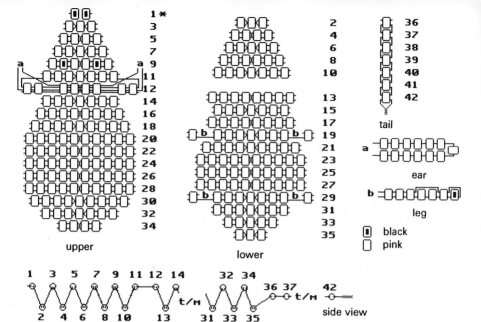

black ▮
pink ☐

upper

lower

tail

ear

leg

side view

25 *Pig pattern*

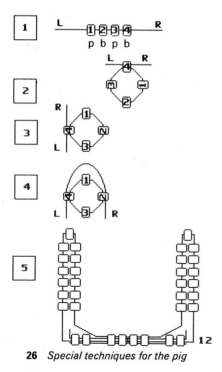

26 *Special techniques for the pig*

the left wire and take the wire through row 12, skipping the first two beads. Work the right side in the same way. From row 12 (upper) continue working in the V-technique up to and including row 36 (upper). In rows 19 and 29 (both lower) the legs are made. Thread the first bead of row 19 and using the same wire make the leg (see pattern). Thread 6 pink beads and 1 black bead, make a loop around the black bead, take the wire back through the first pink bead. Skip the next two pink beads—this creates the effect of a hoof—and take the wire through the next three pink beads of the leg. This finishes the leg. Continue beading row 19. Take the other wire through the last bead of row 19, make the second leg and take the wire back through the beads of row 19 as well as the bead that is before the leg. The back legs are made in the same manner, using 5 instead of 6 pink beads as they are slightly shorter than the front legs. From row 36, which consists of only one bead, continue up to row 42 inclusive using the flat technique for the tail.

Finishing
Finish all loose wires. Straighten the legs, making sure the black bead is to the front. Curl the tail. Bend the nose up and flatten the ears against the head.

Pig set (page 40)
You will need
- Small beads, 2 mm (grey, black and pink)
- 6 caps (black)
- 6 decorative caps
- 12 strass beads (black)
- 6 pearls, 4 mm (pink)
- 6 pearls, 6 mm (pink)
- 2 pearls, 8 mm (pink)
- Crochet cotton no. 30 (grey)
- Clasp
- Beading wire 0.80 and 0.25 mm
- Lapel pin
- Hairclip
- Brooch pin

Method
Using the pink and black 2 mm beads make seven pigs, two for the necklace, one for the lapel pin, one for the brooch pin and three for the hairclip.

Necklace
For the necklace thread: * 3 pink and 2 grey beads on crochet cotton, repeating from * and making 2 pieces of beaded cord 20 cm (8") long and one piece 8 cm (3") long. Finish each piece of beaded cord at both ends with 0.80 mm beading wire and 1 cap, 1 decorative cap, 1 strass bead and 1 pearl. Make a ring at the end. Attach the pigs to a piece of beading wire and make a ring at both ends. The smaller piece of beaded cord is the centrepiece of the necklace, with a pig at either end, then a long piece of beaded cord either side, finished with a clasp at the back.

Lapel pin
Attach 1 pearl, 1 strass bead, one pig, 1 strass bead and 1 pearl to the lapel pin. Apply a little glue to the last pearl and close the lid of the lapel pin.

Brooch pin
Use 1 pig and 1 brooch pin. Attach the pig to the brooch pin using the thinner beading wire.

Hairclip (Fig. 24)
Cut a piece of beading wire approximately 2 cm (³/₄") longer than the hairclip; attach this to one end of the hairclip. Thread in order 1 pearl 6 mm, 1 strass bead, 1 pearl 8 mm, 1 strass bead, 1 pearl 6 mm, 3 pigs from the side (these will be under the beading wire), 1 pearl 6 mm, 1 strass bead, 1 pearl 8 mm, 1 strass bead and 1 pearl 6 mm. Attach the other end of the beading wire with a ring to the hairclip.

Cat (page 31)

You will need
- 277 small beads, 2 mm (270 black, 7 pink)
- 2 medium beads, 3 mm (green)
- 1.25 m (1¼ yd) beading wire

Method (Fig. 28)
Start at the nose using the setting-up technique and continue working in the V-technique up to row 9 inclusive. The whiskers are made between rows 2 and 3, 3 and 4 and 4 and 5. To make them, leave the wire loose enough for a loop to develop. Each loop is twisted around several times (see Fig. 21 for the mouse). The eyes are beaded in row 5. The ears are made in row 9—thread 10 beads onto the left wire and 7 beads on the right wire. Take the left wire through the first bead of the right wire (i.e. skip 6 beads, wire through first bead). Take the right wire through the last 3 beads and

the first bead. Skip the next 6 beads, which will form the ears.
Continue working in the V-technique to row 16 inclusive. The front legs are made one on either side of row 16. Thread onto the right wire the first bead of row 16. Make the leg following the pattern. Thread one bead onto the left wire and make the leg following the pattern. Thread the leftover beads onto the left wire, then take the right wire through these beads. Take the right wire through the first bead of the left wire (the bead for the leg). Take the left wire through the first bead of the right wire (the bead for the leg).
Continue working in the V-technique to row 28 inclusive. Make the back legs

27 *Cat made with wooden beads*

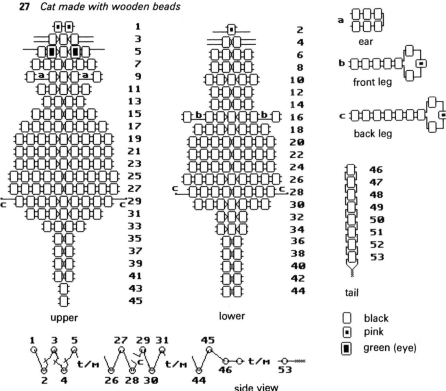

28 *Cat pattern*

following the pattern and continue
working in the V-technique to row 45
inclusive. To make the last piece of the
tail use the flat technique.

Finishing
The whiskers are twisted and cut, allow-
ing the nose to be more flexible. Finish
all loose wires. Move legs and ears into
position and curl the tail.

Frightening animals

Snake (page 31)

You will need
- 479 small beads, 2 mm (226 gold, 244 green, 9 pink)
- 2 medium beads, 3 mm (gold)
- 1.25 m (1¼ yd) beading wire

(These quantities are sufficient to make a small snake; to make a larger snake you will need more small beads.)

Method (Figs 30 and 31)
The snake is started at the tongue. Following Fig. 31 thread 6 pink beads. Fold the wire in the middle and take the left wire back through the second and third beads. Take the right wire back through the fifth and fourth beads (Fig. 31-c). With both wires together thread 3 more beads. With the two wires coming out of the tongue start at row 1; using the V-technique, follow the pattern to row 115 inclusive. The eyes are beaded in row 9. In every third row a gold bead is threaded. The tail starts in row 89, decreasing as shown in the pattern.

Green snake set (page 36)
This set consists of a bracelet, earrings, two brooches, a necklace and a hairclip.

You will need
- Pearls, 4 mm (green, gold and cream)
- Variety of clasps (e.g. hook and eye)
- 2 oval caps, 18 mm

29 *Snake earring*

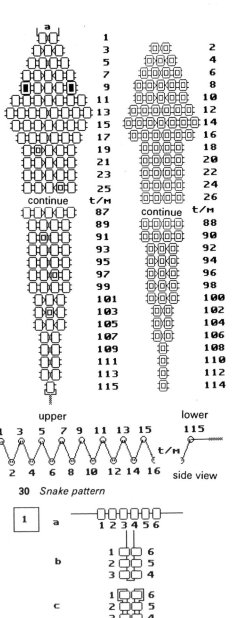

a

tongue

	light green
X	pink
⊙	gold
■	gold (eyes)

30 Snake pattern

31 Pattern for the snake's tongue

- Small beads, 2 mm (pink)
- Beading wire 0.30 and 0.80 mm
- Small brooch pin
- Beads for the eyes (8 mm)
- 2 perforated disc brooches (1 oval and 1 pointed oval)
- Hairclip and earrings

Bracelet
Make two snakes up to and including row 47. Connect the two backs by taking the wire from one back and working it into the last row of the other back. Attach the fastening to the head of the snake, under the tongue.

Earrings
Make two snakes' heads, working up to and including row 19, and fasten these to the perforated disc earrings.

Brooch with three snakes' heads
Make three snakes' heads, working up to and including row 21, and fasten them to the pointed oval brooch. Fill the perforated holes in the disc with gold 4 mm pearls.

Brooch with movable snake
Make a full length snake, or increase the length slightly by adding several rows (still using 4 mm pearls). Attach a perforated oval disc brooch to the head and

a brooch pin to the tail. With the disc brooch and the brooch pin fastened some distance away from each other, the snake can be adjusted to any position required.

Hairclip

Make two snakes, working up to and including row 23, and fasten the bodies together. Cut a piece of 0.80 mm beading wire approximately 2 cm (5/8") longer than the hairclip. Attach this to one end of the hairclip, slide the double snake on and fasten the wire to the other end of the hairclip.

Necklace

Make two snakes each 25 cm (10") long. Join the heads together with beading wire. Attach an oval cap and a fastening at each end.

Black snake set (Fig. 32)

This set consists of a belt, a brooch and two earrings.

You will need

- Gold elasticised belt with perforated disc fastenings
- Pearls, 4 mm (gold and black)
- Pearls, 8 mm (gold and black)

32 *Black snake set*

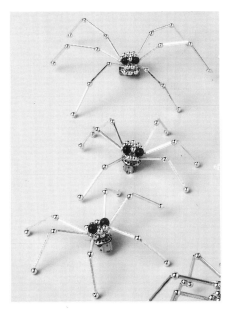

33 *Spider set*

- 6 pearls, 12 mm, for the eyes (gold)
- 27 pearls, 3 mm, for the tongue (gold)
- 18 pearls, 2 mm, for the tongue (gold)
- A pair of perforated disc earrings
- Perforated disc brooch

Method
Make three large snake heads for the belt and brooch using 8 mm pearls, with 12 mm pearls for the eyes and 3 mm pearls for the tongues, following the pattern up to and including row 19. The earrings are made as described for the green snake set, using 4 mm pearls with 8 mm pearls for the eyes and 2 mm pearls for the tongue, working to and including row 19.

Belt and brooch
Attach one of the snake heads to the brooch and two to the perforated discs of the belt. Fill the rest of the disc with gold beads and strass beads at the sides.

Earrings
Make up as described for the green snake set.

Spider (page 31)

You will need
- 38 small beads, 2 mm (light brown)
- 2 medium beads, 3 mm (dark brown)
- 18 bugle beads (gold)
- 0.75 m (30") beading wire

Method (Fig. 34)
Begin the spider following the setting-up technique for rows 1 and 2. The eyes are beaded in row 2. The left wire coming out of row 2 will form the left leg. Thread 1 bugle, 1 bead, 1 bugle, 1 bead, 1 bugle and 1 bead, make a loop around the last bead and take the wire back through the rest of the beads of the leg. Make the right leg in the same manner.

The wires coming out of both legs will form row 3 (lower). Row 4 (lower) is connected using the flat technique. From row 4 use the V-technique up to and including row 7. Between rows 4 and 5 make both the middle legs b, between rows 6 and 7 make both the back legs c. The two wires coming out of row 7 are twisted together and finished in the work.

Finishing
Finish all loose wires. Adjust the legs to the right shape.

Spider earrings and brooch (Fig. 33)
You will need
- Pearls, 4 mm (silver)
- Beads, 6 mm (black)
- Bugle beads, 2.5 cm
- Beading wire 0.30 mm
- 2 perforated disc earrings, 18 mm
- Perforated disc brooch with a diameter of 20 mm (5/8")

Method
Make three silver spiders with black eyes. Attach one to each of the earrings and one to the brooch. Cover the rest of the perforated disc with beads.

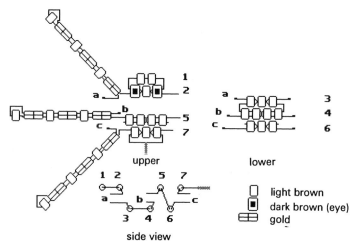

light brown
dark brown (eye)
gold

34 *Spider pattern*

Scorpion (page 31)

You will need
- 177 small beads, 2 mm (24 anthracite, 67 light grey, 86 beige)
- 2 medium beads, 3 mm (light brown)
- 28 bugle beads (gold)
- 1.5 m (1½ yd) beading wire

35 *Scorpion made with wooden beads*

Method (Fig. 36)
The scorpion is started at the tail following the setting up technique (rows 1 and 2). Continue working in the flat technique to row 11 inclusive. The two wires coming out of row 11 are taken to the upper side of the work using the U-technique and together form row 12. The two wires coming out of row 12 together form row 13 on the upper side. The two wires coming out of row 13 are taken to the lower side and together form row 14. Repeat rows 11 to 14 up to row 23 inclusive (row 23 is on the lower side). The wire coming out of the left side of row 23 will form leg a on the left side. To make the leg, thread 1 bugle, 1 bead, 1 bugle, 1 bead, 1 bugle and 3 beads. Make a loop around the last bead and take the wire back through the rest of the leg. The wire coming out of the right side of row 23 will form leg a on the right side; both wires coming out of the legs (left and right) form row 24 (upper side). The two wires coming out of row 24 together form row 25 (upper side). The wire coming out of the left side of row 25 will form the left leg b. The wire coming out of the right side of row 25 will form right leg b. The two wires (left and right) coming out of the legs form row 26 (lower side). Continue following the pattern to row 33 inclusive, beading the eyes in row 32 in the medium sized beads.

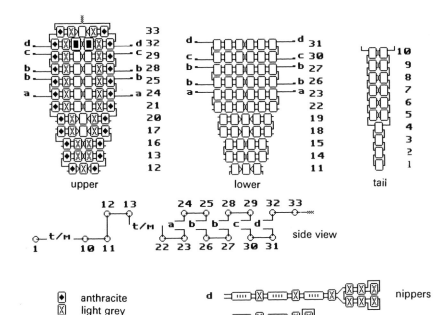

upper   lower   taii

side view

	anthracite
	light grey
	light brown (eyes)
	beige
	gold

d   nippers

c

b

a   legs

36 *Scorpion pattern*

Finishing
Finish all loose wires. Bend the legs into shape. Raise the two nippers and bend the tail up and curl it.

Crab (page 31)

You will need
- 110 small beads, 2 mm (salmon coloured)
- 2 medium beads, 3 mm (purple)
- 20 bugle beads (red)
- 1 m (1 yd) beading wire

Method (Fig. 38)
The crab has many combinations of connections. (It might be a good idea to read the last part of the V-technique again.)

The crab is started from underneath with row 1 (lower side), working in the U-technique to row 6 (upper) inclusive. In the connections between rows 3 and 4 and rows 5 and 6 the legs are made. Continue working using the V-technique

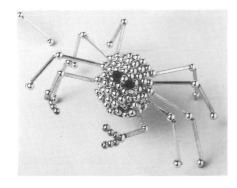

37 *Part of the crab set*

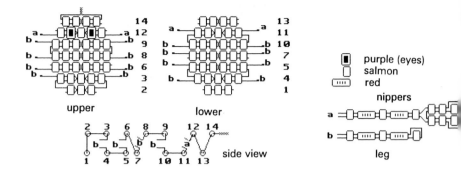

upper

lower

side view

| purple (eyes) |
| salmon |
| red |

nippers

leg

38 *Crab pattern*

to row 8 inclusive. From row 8 to row 11 inclusive continue working in the U-technique. Between rows 7 and 8 and between rows 9 and 10 make more legs. From row 11 continue using the V-technique to row 14 inclusive. In the connection between rows 11 and 12 make the claws. The eyes are beaded in row 12.

Finishing
Finish all loose wires. Raise the claws and bend all the legs into shape.

Crab set (Fig. 37)
You will need
- Pearls no. 3 (white)
- Bugle beads, 2 cm (satin white)
- Faceted beads (silver)
- Perforated disc earrings
- Beading wire 0.25 mm
- Perforated disc brooch

Brooch
Make a crab following the pattern and fasten onto a perforated disc brooch.

Earrings
For each earring you will need 'half' a crab. Follow the pattern, but for one earring leave out the two left beads of the pattern, as well as the legs and claws on the left side. For the other earring leave out the same beads, but on the

right side. Attach the crabs to the perforated discs, making a left and a right earring.

Bee (page 31)

You will need
- 29 small beads, 2 mm (2 black, 11 dark brown, 16 yellow)
- 2 medium beads, 3 mm (black)
- 0.75 m (30") beading wire

Method (Fig. 39)
Start at the top by making the nose. Thread 2 black beads which are connected using the flat technique to row 2. Rows 2, 3 and 4 are made in the U-technique. From row 4 continue using the V-technique up to row 10 inclusive. The eyes are beaded in row 5. Between rows 5 and 6, rows 6 and 7 and rows 7 and 8 the wings are made. The wires are not pulled tight but left to create a loop. These loops are twisted around several times (see Fig. 21 for the mouse), but are not cut, as this time they form the wings.

Finishing
Finish all loose wires. Make sure the wings are rounded and overlap slightly.

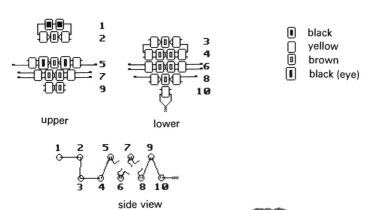

	black
	yellow
	brown
	black (eye)

upper   lower

side view

39 *Bee pattern*

40 *Bee set*

Black bee set (Fig. 40)

Earrings
You will need
- Pearls, 3 mm (black and multicoloured)
- 4 beads, 4 mm for the eyes (gold, faceted)
- Small beads, 2 mm (black)
- Perforated disc earrings

Method
Make two bees and fasten them to the perforated disc earrings. The wing wires are not left bare, but are each beaded with 40 black 2 mm beads before being twisted and fixed in place. Cover any bare areas of the perforated discs with beads.

Brooch
You will need
- Pearls, 4 mm (black and multicoloured)
- Faceted beads (5 mm) for the eyes (gold)
- Small beads, 2 mm (black)
- Perforated disc brooch

Method
Make one bee, using 80 black 2 mm beads for each wing, and attach this to the brooch. Cover the rest of the perforations with beads.

Yellow and black bee set (Fig. 41)
You will need
- Small beads, 2 mm (yellow, black)
- Pearls, 2 mm (gold)
- 5 pieces of chain 5 cm (2") long (gold)
- 4 pieces of chain 3 cm (1¼") long (gold)
- 1 piece of chain 50 cm (20") long (gold)
- Rings
- Long lapel pin
- Beading wire 0.25 mm
- Pair of earring hangers
- Clasp
- Decorative beads

Method
Using the bee pattern, make 14 black and yellow bees with gold eyes, and twisted wire wings.

Earrings
The earrings are made using pieces of chain. Each earring has two pieces of chain 5 cm (2") and one piece of chain 3 cm (1¼"). Attach one bee to each piece of chain. Attach the pieces of chain to the earring hanger.

Necklace
Attach a ring to each of five bees and attach each ring to the 50 cm (20") chain. Fit the clasp to the end of the chain.

Lapel pin
Attach three bees to a piece of chain 5 cm (2") long and two pieces 3 cm (1¼") long. Decorate some headpins with beads and form a ring in the ends. Thread the chains and headpins decoratively onto the lapel pin and bend the lapel pin back to finish.

Ant-lion (page 31)

You will need
- 93 small beads, 2 mm (11 brown, 82 yellow)
- 2 medium beads, 3 mm (red)
- 8 bugle beads (brown)
- 0.75 m (30") beading wire

Method
The ant-lion is started at the back on the lower layer (rows 1 and 2) using the setting-up technique. Use the flat technique to make row 3. The left wire coming out of row 3 forms the left leg a, the right wire coming out of row 3 forms the right leg a. Both wires coming out of the legs together form row 4. Continue using the flat technique to row 6 inclusive.

41 *Yellow and black bee set*

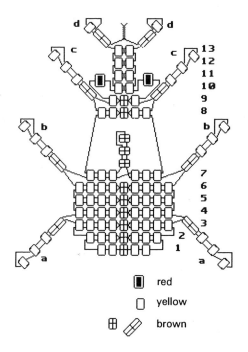

technique to row 13 inclusive. The left wire coming out of row 13 forms the left antenna d, the right wire coming out of row 13 forms the right antenna d. The two wires (left and right) coming from the antennae are used to finish off the work.

Finishing
Finish all loose wires. All six legs are bent down. The antennae can be bent up or down as required.

■ red

☐ yellow

⊞ ⬚ brown

42 *Ant-lion pattern*

The left wire coming out of row 6 will form the left leg b, the right wire coming out of row 6 will form the right leg b. The two wires coming from the legs together form row 7. In the middle of row 7 make an antenna, which needs to stand up. The space indicated in the pattern is only there to demonstrate the antenna—in reality row 8 is beaded directly against row 7.
The left wire coming out of row 8 will form the left leg c, the right wire coming out of row 8 forms right leg c. The two wires coming out of the legs together form row 9.
The eyes are made between rows 8 and 9 using 3 mm beads.
From row 10 continue working in the flat